MARCOS AND THE PHILIPPINES

MARCOS

AND THE PHILIPPINES

DON LAWSON

FRANKLIN WATTS
New York ▪ London ▪ Toronto ▪ Sidney
AN IMPACT BOOK ▪ 1984

Map by Vantage Art, Inc.

Photographs courtesy of:
UPI/Bettmann Archive: pp. 3, 17, 34, 39, 48, 66, 72;
IAEA/Goldberger: p. 20; National Archives: p. 54;
MacArthur Memorial: p. 65.

Library of Congress Cataloging in Publication Data

Lawson, Don.
Marcos and the Philippines.

(An Impact book)
Bibliography: p.
Includes index.
Summary: Presents a brief history of the Philippines
and discusses the dictatorship of President Marcos and
the present political controversy which surrounds it.
Offers speculations about the future of this troubled
country.
1. Philippines—Politics and government—1946- —
Juvenile literature. 2. Marcos, Ferdinand E. (Ferdinand
Edralin), 1917- —Juvenile literature. [1. Philippines
—Politics and government. 2. Marcos, Ferdinand E.
(Ferdinand Edralin), 1917-   ] I. Title.
DS686.5.L3 1984   959.9'04   84-7542
ISBN 0-531-04856-X

CONTENTS

CHAPTER I
The Assassination of Benigno Aquino 1

CHAPTER II
Facts About the Philippines 11

CHAPTER III
Who Is Ferdinand Marcos? 29

CHAPTER IV
Early History of the Philippines 43

CHAPTER V
Modern History of the Philippines 57

CHAPTER VI
The Future of the Philippines 69

Bibliography 83

Index 85

To Estelle Murphy,
Respected Researcher
and Co-Worker in the
Editorial Vineyard

I

THE ASSASSINATION OF BENIGNO AQUINO

On a hot, sunny day in late August 1983, a jumbo jet airplane bearing a very important passenger landed at Manila airport in the Philippines. The VIP was Benigno Aquino, a former Filipino senator. Aquino was returning to his homeland after three long years of exile in the United States.

As soon as the plane landed, it was boarded by an armed military escort. Aquino had received several threats against his life when he had announced that he was returning to the Philippines. Members of the government's Aviation Security Command were supposedly provided to protect Aquino against any attempts to assassinate him.

Exactly what happened in the first few moments after his plane landed has been the subject of controversy ever since.

What is definitely known is that just seconds after Aquino walked down the steps from the plane accompanied by his escort, he was shot through the head and died instantly. Moments later a whole volley of shots rang out, and another man lay dead on the tarmac, or runway. This man was later identified as Rolando Galman who, authorities claimed, had murdered Aquino and who was in turn gunned down by Aquino's military escort.

But civilian eyewitnesses to the twin killings claimed otherwise. They insisted that Aquino had been shot by one of his escorts who was on the ramp behind him. They also said that after Aquino had been shot, the already lifeless body of Galman had been pushed out the back door of a van onto the tarmac and that one of Aquino's escorts had then emptied his carbine into the body of the dead "assassin."

And who was to blame for this brutal execution? The finger of suspicion seemed to point to no less a person than the president of the Philippines, Ferdinand Marcos, or at least to members of Marcos' overzealous top military command.

Marcos has been president of the Philippines for some eighteen years, even though the Republic's original constitution said that no president was permitted to serve for more than two consecutive four-year terms. In 1972, Marcos proclaimed a new constitution with himself as president and prime minister (the constitution was formally adopted in 1973) and had then imposed martial law throughout the country. This meant that civil authority had been done away with and the military forces took over all law-enforcement responsibilities.

But the Philippines has a long tradition of democracy, and there has been much opposition to Marcos' military dictatorship. One of the leaders of this opposition was Benigno Aquino. So troublesome had Aquino's political opposition become that Marcos had him thrown in military prison. Marcos finally agreed to release Aquino so that Aquino could go to the United States for heart surgery. Aquino promised he would one day return.

*Benigno Aquino (in white)
and his alleged assassin
lie dead on the tarmac
at the Manila airport.*

During Aquino's stay in the United States, home opposition to Marcos' dictatorial rule grew stronger. Marcos finally promised to hold free parliamentary elections in "the near future." Marcos himself was not up for reelection, but it was rumored that he was in poor health and that he, too, might step down. Aquino decided that the time was now ripe for a return to his homeland and resumption of his political opposition to Marcos. He planned to take part in the 1984 elections and to organize the democratic non-Communist opposition. He also said he intended to try to negotiate with Marcos for a return to a constitutional democracy.

Friends, family, even political allies warned Aquino not to return. President Marcos told Aquino that if he returned, he would surely be marked for death by forces beyond the government's control. Despite these warnings, Aquino did return, and now lay dead—the most recent in a long series of martyrs who have attempted to establish and maintain a democratic government in the Philippines.

MARCOS APPOINTS AN
INVESTIGATION COMMITTEE

There was violent public reaction to Aquino's assassination. "Ninoy," as he was affectionately called, had been a greatly loved figure among all freedom-loving Filipinos. Rumors that he had been gunned down on orders of his chief political rival, Ferdinand Marcos, caused riots to erupt throughout the Philippines.

To quell the disorders, Marcos announced that he would appoint an "impartial" committee to investigate the slaying. However, when the committee was named, it proved to be made up mainly of Marcos supporters and henchmen. Chairman of the five-member committee was Philippine Supreme Court Justice Enrique M. Fernando. When his impartiality was legally challenged, Fernando resigned. Marcos promptly named a new chairman, Arturo Tolentino, a member of Marcos' ruling party. He, too, was publicly challenged and did not accept the post. The other members of the investigation committee resigned. Marcos promised that a new and "truly impartial" investigative panel would be named in the near future. Opposition leaders quickly rejected the idea that any government panel would be able to reach an objective, unbiased conclusion.

"The whole trouble is that Marcos is the first suspect," said Agapito Aquino, brother of the slain former senator. "As long as Marcos is in power, there can be no fair and independent investigation."

Meanwhile, pressure for an honest disclosure of the facts surrounding the assassination was being brought to bear on Marcos by the United States. Although the Philippines is an independent republic, it still has strong historic and economic ties with the United States. In addition, U.S. President Ronald Reagan planned to make a state visit to the Philippines in early November. Cancellation of this visit would be a sharp blow to Marcos' political future, which for the first time in more than a decade was somewhat in doubt.

A new five-member board opened its hearings at the end of October. It was headed by a judge, Justice Corazon Agrava, and included three lawyers and the chairman of the Philippine Chamber of Commerce. The testimony heard—mainly from military officers—continued to point to Rolando Galman as the assassin. Galman, it was claimed, was a revolutionary and a communist and a former guerrilla who had been a long-time political enemy of Aquino's.

According to members of Aquino's military escort, Galman had apparently been hiding behind the ramp stairway of the aircraft from which Aquino had descended. When Aquino reached the bottom step, they testified, Galman ducked out from behind the ramp and at close quarters fired a single shot from a magnum revolver, hitting Aquino in the head. The weapon was found on the tarmac beside the body of the slain assassin.

But according to both eyewitness and expert testimony, there were many flaws in this version of the facts. Aquino had indeed been killed by a single shot in the head, which entered behind the left ear. The bullet, however, traveled *downward,* exiting at the chin. If Galman, a man no taller than Aquino, had indeed attempted the assassination, he would not have been in a position at ground level to fire his weapon from the indicated angle. But several members of Aquino's military escort *were* in such a position; at least two of them were on the ramp steps behind him. Eyewitnesses also continued to insist that Galman had not emerged from behind the ramp but that his lifeless body had been pitched from the van onto the tarmac. Some sixteen shots had been fired into Galman from the front, but there were also two bullet wounds in his back.

Additional testimony was also given to the effect that gunpowder was found on the hands of two members of the military escort. The government insisted, however, that the escort had not been armed with handguns or revolvers, only small rifles called carbines.

By year's end, no wholly satisfactory solution to the killing had yet been offered, but the Philippines government announced its official conclusion—that Galman was the slayer.

Meanwhile, the mass demonstrations continued throughout the Republic, and in the face of this unrest President Reagan canceled his visit.

IMPORTANCE OF THE PHILIPPINES TO THE UNITED STATES

The cancellation of the presidential visit was not done without considerable soul-searching in Washington.

The Philippines, after all, is one of America's most important strategic military outposts in the Pacific, and it is vital that the United States retain the Filipino president as an ally. There is, to be sure, serious question as to how long the Marcos regime can remain in power, so it is also politically important not to alienate Marcos' opposition, which might soon take over the Philippine government.

As was expected, many Filipinos hailed the cancellation of the presidential trip as a sign of support for the opposition. Marcos, on the other hand, expressed his surprise and keen disappointment. Not only had he guaranteed Reagan's safety during the planned visit, but he had also pledged various political reforms to quiet the general unrest. He also reminded the U.S. government of a statement made just a short time earlier by U.S. Vice President George Bush that praised Marcos for his fight to promote democracy in the Philippines.

But Marcos was well aware that he had to tread softly and not be too critical of the decision. He badly needed American support to remain in power. He also desperately needed the vast sums of money the United States was giving him to bolster his country's sagging economy.

This money on which the Philippines has long been dependent comes from both American government and business grants and loans. In addition, two major U.S. military installations in the Philippines add vast sums annually to the Republic's coffers. Since the Philippines already owes at least $22 billion borrowed from foreign countries—mainly the United States—it was in the interest of both Marcos and the Reagan administration that no drastic moves be made that might lead to this debt not being paid back. If the Philippines were to default on this debt, that is fail to pay it back, all future U.S. economic aid to that country would stop. On its part, the United States would not only lose all the money already loaned, but the Philippines might also take over the two military bases there and even lease them to somebody else—perhaps the Soviet Union.

The two U.S. military installations that are so important to both the Philippines and the United States are the Subic Bay Naval Base and Clark Air Force Base, two of the largest American bases outside the United States. Together these bases are occupied by more than sixteen thousand service personnel and provide major support for U.S. military activities in both the Pacific and Indian oceans.

In the spring of 1983, the United States government renewed an agreement with the Philippines government that involves paying "rent" on these bases to the tune of $900 million over the next five years. In addition, the two bases provide jobs for some forty thousand Filipinos that amounts to about $300 million in wages, there are a variety of service contracts, and there is the money spent in the Philippines by U.S. service men and women. Although costly, this marriage of convenience was regarded as an excellent bargain—in fact a virtual Philippine "giveaway"—by most international experts.

The huge naval base at Subic Bay on the western coast of Luzon Island and nearby Clark Air Force Base together serve as a military security shield for the United States and its allies in a region that has recently seen an enormous military build-up by the Soviet Union. Together the two bases form a vital defense link from the Philippines to Japan and Korea to the eastern coast of Australia. Westward, the defense line runs into the Indian Ocean and the Persian Gulf, through which oil supplies vital to the Western world are transported.

Clark Air Force Base, with its 8,700 service men and women is the home of the Thirteenth Air Force and several fighter units of the Pacific Air Force, whose headquarters are in Hawaii. Clark also provides air support for U.S. naval operations in the Indian Ocean and the Persian Gulf.

The Subic Bay base, with its 7,500 U.S. personnel, is a major supply and ship repair facility. It provides support for the U.S. Seventh Fleet, whose ships operate throughout the Western Pacific and the Indian Ocean. There is also a naval airfield at Subic Bay, which is the land base for the Seventh Fleet's aircraft carrier strike force.

It is estimated that it would cost between $8 billion and $10 billion to relocate these two vital military bases elsewhere in the Pacific. And from a strategic military standpoint, located elsewhere—say, on Guam—they would not be as ideally situated as they are now. Ships and planes would have much greater distances to travel at any other location, and there would be other negative factors—not the least of which would be the loss of the skilled, low-paid Filipino work force.

But even if the Marcos regime is toppled and Marcos' political opponents come to power, it is not believed by analysts of the situation that there is any real threat to the U.S. military bases in the Philippines. Consequently, the Philippines will doubtless continue to be a key Pacific bastion for the United States as it has been since the turn of the twentieth century.

GROWING SOVIET POWER IN ASIA

Since the end of the Vietnam War in the early 1970s, the Soviet Union has gradually expanded its military capability in Asia by using Vietnam as a base for its naval and air operations. One of the key Vietnamese installations taken over by the Russians was the former U.S. base at Cam Ranh Bay, which the United States was forced to abandon when it lost the Vietnam War.

Late in 1983, the Soviets deployed offensive bombers at Cam Ranh Bay with a roundtrip range of 3,000 miles (4,800 km). These bombers, called TU16s or Badgers, are capable of reaching numerous U.S. installations in the region, including those in the Philippines. Also stationed at Cam Ranh Bay are Soviet nuclear-powered, nuclear-armed submarines, as well as surface and support ships, that present a clear threat to the United States and its allies throughout the Far East.

Officials at Clark Air Force Base and Subic Bay Naval Base, as well as those at the Pentagon in Washington, regard the Soviet buildup in Vietnam as ominous. They point out, however, that the United States should remain more than an even match for the Russians in Asia as long as it keeps its guard up. This situation, however, has caused heightened concern on the part of the U.S. government regarding the ongoing political unrest in the Philippines.

II

FACTS ABOUT
THE
PHILIPPINES

The Republic of the Philippines is made up of a long string of some 7,100 mountainous islands in the southwestern Pacific Ocean area off the coast of Southeast Asia. The main group of islands from Luzon in the north to Mindanao in the south is about 1,000 miles (1,600 km) long and 300 miles (480 km) wide. The approximate land area is 115,830 square miles (300,000 sq km). This is roughly the size of Arizona or Illinois and Wisconsin combined. The United States is 6,000 miles (9,600 km) to the northeast.

The population (1982 *World Almanac*) was 51,600,000.

The ten major islands are Luzon, Mindanao, Samar, Negros, Palawan, Panay, Mindoro, Leyte, Cebu, and Bohol. They range in size from Luzon, which is 40,420 square miles (105,092 sq km), down to Bohol, which is 1,492 square miles (3,879 sq km). The smallest island among the fewer than twenty that are inhabited is Siquijor, with an area of 129 square miles (335 sq km).

ITBAYAT

SABTANG

PACIFIC
OCEAN

BABUYAN ISLANDS

SOUTH
CHINA
SEA

Palanan

LUZON

SIERRA MADRE

PHILIPPINE
SEA

Tarlac
Concepcion
Clark Air Force Base
Subic Bay Naval Base
Malolos
Bataan Peninsula
Manila
Quezon City
CORREGIDOR
Manila Bay

MINDORO

SAMAR

MASBATE

PANAY
Iloilo

Tacloban
LEYTE
Leyte Gulf

Bacolod

Cebu
CEBU
BOHOL

PALAWAN

NEGROS

SIQUIJOR

SULU SEA

MINDANAO

Davao

Zamboanga

CELEBES
SEA

MAJOR CITIES

The capital of the Philippines is Manila, with a 1980 population of 1,626,249. The population of the entire Manila metropolitan area, however, is almost six million.

The old capital is Quezon City, northeast of Manila, with a population of 1,165,990.

Other important cities and their populations include Davao on Mindanao, 611,311; Zamboanga, also on Mindanao, 344,275; Cebu on Cebu Island, 489,208; Bacolod on Negros, 266,604; Iloilo on Panay, 244,211; and Tarlac on Luzon, 121,400.

CLIMATE AND CROPS

The climate of the Philippines is tropical. Rainfall is generally heavy but seasonal, with most of the rain falling between June and November. Precipitation ranges from 50 to 180 inches (125 to 450 cm) a year, depending on the location. Most of the rain falls in the uplands. The lowlands lie in what is called a "rain shadow," with the upland mountains blocking off the moisture-filled air from the ocean.

The late summer and early autumn months between August and October often bring destructive typhoons to the islands. These fierce storms strike most frequently north of Manila. The Philippines is also subject to violent earthquakes, most of them occurring on Mindanao.

Because of the generally fertile soil found in the lowlands and on the mountain slopes, and the year-round warm-to-moderate temperatures, the Philippines is rich in many agricultural products. These include rice, corn, bananas, citrus fruits, nuts, various root crops, coconuts, tobacco, sisal (hemp), and sugar cane. The Philippines is a world leader in coconut production, and its hemp is the best natural fiber available. During World War II, when Japan occupied the Philippines, the world shortage of hemp caused serious packaging problems, especially in the United States and Great Britain. Today, plastic cord is widely used in place of hemp—even in Filipino fishermen's nets. In the upland areas, vast forests supply timber and other forest products. Philippine mahogany is famous throughout the world.

LANGUAGES AND RELIGION

There are several major languages spoken in the Philippines. Among them are Pilipino, Tagalog, English, and Spanish. Since 1946, Pilipino has been the official language of the Republic. It is based on Tagalog, which is a Malayan dialect. About half the people speak English, and a number of them also speak Spanish. English and Spanish are commonly used for government and commercial purposes. In addition, there are at least seventy-five native languages and dialects spoken throughout the islands.

Religion is a significant factor in the Philippines. At least eighty percent of the population is Roman Catholic, and several million people are Protestant. This makes it the only predominantly Christian nation in Asia. Members of minority religions include Moslems, Buddhists, and others. The fact that the Philippine population is mainly Catholic and that Catholicism is opposed to birth control has resulted in a very high birth rate and severe overpopulation problems in the Philippines.

GOVERNMENT

The United States governed the Philippines from the end of the Spanish-American War in the late 1890s to the end of World War II in the mid-1940s. The Republic gained its independence on July 4, 1946. Since then, the Filipinos have experienced a rocky road to freedom and democracy, one marked by occasional peasant revolutions, riotous demonstrations by students and workers, and despotic one-man rule in the person of its current president, Ferdinand Marcos.

During the latter years of U.S. colonialism in the Philippines, the country was allowed to prepare for independence. It adopted a constitution patterned after the U.S. Constitution and instituted voting reforms.

First adopted in 1935, the original Philippine constitution had two features that distinguished it from the U.S. Constitution. It provided for a single, six-year term for the president, and there was only a single house (unicameral) legislature. In 1940, these features were eliminated by amendment. In 1946, when independence was declared, further amendments were made. Each of these amendments was aimed at decentralizing the government by decreasing the power of the president and giving more authority directly to the people in the seventy-three provinces.

Under the 1946 constitution, there was a president and vice president, both of whom were to be elected by popular vote to four-year terms. The president was not permitted to serve for more than two consecutive terms.

There was also a two-house legislature, the Senate and House of Representatives. The judicial system was headed by an eleven-member Supreme Court, with the chief justice and the associate justices appointed by the president. A system of lower courts, also similar to that in the United States, was provided for the provinces, municipalities, chartered cities, and *barrios*, or rural villages.

Civil administration in each of the provinces was headed by a governor and two other board members. Municipalities and chartered cities were to have mayor-council governments, and the barrios had limited local control of their own affairs.

Under this constitutional system, the government of the Philippines worked moderately well as a democracy until 1965, when Marcos came to power. A two-party political system, the Nationalist and Liberal parties, dominated Philippine politics. Unfortunately, there was little actual difference in their ideas about how to run the government. Filipino voters had a tendency to vote for political leaders with powerful personalities rather than for able administrators. Also unfortunately, both fraud—vote stealing, dishonest vote counting, false voter registrations, etc.—and violence became common in Philippine politics.

Reform movements were started to eliminate political fraud and violence, but third parties have had very little success in Philippine politics. Marcos promised to create his own brand of reform—a common promise made by all potential political dictators—if he were given enough power.

By way of taking all authority into his own hands, Marcos abolished the vice-presidency. He then had himself named both president and prime minister, and the two-term presidential provision was abolished. Technically, this was legal, since it was part of the Marcos constitution adopted in 1973. To further establish his "legal" right to remain in power under this new document, Marcos held a rigged referendum in 1977 in which "no" notes were simply not counted correctly. His declaration of martial law, however, continued to cause unrest, so he formally lifted it in 1981 and gave the legislative assembly limited rights to pass certain legislation. He also released political prisoners—among them Benigno Aquino—and promised to no longer rule by decree. In June of that year, he was reelected president for a six-year term.

Once he gained the presidency,
Marcos set about concentrating
all government power firmly in his
own hands. In this 1971 photo, university
students protest the increasingly
dictatorial Marcos administration.

Soon after his reelection, however, Marcos resumed his old dictatorial ways. The legislative assembly became a rubber stamp, automatically approving Marcos' demand decrees without debate, and the military once again was called on to enforce the so-called law. Throughout the islands, the judiciary was no longer called on to decide legal disputes, since the military had taken the law into its own hands.

Today, the Philippines is a democracy in name only. Technically, all male and female citizens of fifteen years of age or older who can read and write are entitled to vote in local, provincial, and national elections. But when those elections, especially at the national level, are either rigged by fraudulent voting or nonexistent, voting becomes an exercise in futility. The fact that Marcos received 88 percent of the vote in the 1981 presidential election was not so much a sign of his popularity as it was an indication that any and all opposition to him was ruthlessly suppressed.

Today, and no doubt for as long as Marcos or his handpicked successor remains in power, the government of the Republic of the Philippines is a military dictatorship. It is this situation that reformer Benigno Aquino hoped to have a hand in changing when he returned to the Philippines. And it is just such reform that Marcos and his political henchmen apparently cannot and will not tolerate.

THE FILIPINO WAY OF LIFE

Most Filipinos are of Malaysian descent. A few thousand, perhaps fifteen thousand, are dark-skinned Negritos and are considered to be non-Malaysian. Among the Malaysians there are many ancestral divisions. These range from the Cebuanos and Tagalogs—the two largest divisions—to the Pampangos and Ilongos, which are among the smallest.

Many Filipinos also have Chinese, Hindu, Spanish, and American ancestors. At least a million are part Chinese.

Population growth is a serious problem in the Philippines. In the past decade, population has increased at an annual rate of from 3 to 3.5 percent, one of the highest in the world. In a poor country with limited ways of making a living, such overpopulation creates serious social as well as political problems—problems that the Marcos government has failed to solve. Some of these problems are described below.

Most of the people live in rural villages called *barrios* or *barangays*. (Only about 20 percent live in the cities.) The barrio or barangay is similar to an American township. Several barrios make up a *municipio* (municipality), and the commercial and administrative center— similar to a county seat—of a municipio is called a *pablacion.*

Earning a Living

Most Filipinos are farmers and live in rude huts made of bamboo and thatch. Since these can be easily destroyed by typhoons, many farm families try to earn and save enough money to be able to build a home made of cement blocks. An all-wooden home with a corrugated tin roof is something only the most well-to-do villagers can hope to attain. Electricity for illumination is rare. A single, unshaded light bulb dangling from a cord in each room is a luxury.

The average farm family income is less than $500 a year, which is considered well below the national poverty level, which is about $1,200 a year. Rice and corn are the two most important crops. Sweet potatos, yams, peanuts, cassava, and taro are grown for use in case the rice and corn crops fail. Family garden plots may also include stringbeans, tomatoes, onions, and other vegetables.

Until recent years, rice, which is the main food for three-quarters of the population, had to be imported. Today, the Philippines is a rice-exporting nation. This was brought about through the use of new, high-yield rice strains, irrigation projects, fertilizers, and pesticides. These technological advances were made possible by the Marcos administration, which borrowed billions of dollars, mainly from the United States, to improve the life of the Filipino farmer.

Through the U.S. Agency for International Development (AID), money has also been made available for new irrigation projects, to help make the land more productive. Since the 1970s, annual rice harvests have increased from an average of 1.5 to 3.3 tons for each hectare (2.4 acres). This means that many families can sell much of their rice for cash instead of using their harvest simply to feed themselves.

Nevertheless, poverty still persists. In fact, it seems to be growing even worse. In 1971, shortly before Marcos declared martial law, 44 percent of all Filipinos lived at or below the national poverty level. Today, 64 percent are below that level.

Why Poverty Persists

One of the main reasons for the continuing poverty is that there is simply not enough land for each farm family. In an attempt to remedy this situation, Marcos used much of the money he borrowed from other countries to buy millions of acres of land from landlords with large holdings. This land was then turned over to former tenant farmers, who were given low-interest government

This scientist is applying a special fertilizer to the rice crop at an experimental farm in the Philippines.

loans. But the exploding population growth still causes land to be scarce.

A farmer, for example, whose father owned seven hectares (17 acres) of land would divide that land among his seven children. This would give each child a single hectare on which to grow rice and corn. But each of those seven children might in turn have seven or more children, leaving virtually no land to be passed on to the next generation. This is typical of the land-owning situation in rural areas today.

Corruption and inflation also drained off much of the money Marcos borrowed. Officials from the national level on down to the barrio level have all been guilty of appropriating some of the foreign funds for themselves. This has added to the unrest and resentment of the Marcos government. The meteoric rise in the price of oil also caused the cost of fertilizers to increase enormously, since many fertilizers are actually petroleum products.

Even the cost of simple necessities has risen dramatically. Many farm families use kerosene for lamps to light their homes. A decade ago, a litre of kerosene cost one centavo (a tenth of a cent). Today, a litre of this fuel costs one peso and 70 centavos (17 cents).

The high cost of fuel has also sharply reduced the use of farm machinery. Few families or even groups of families could ever afford the initial investment needed to buy a tractor, but formerly one could be rented for a few pesos a day. Today, it costs the equivalent of $2 a day to rent such equipment—a prohibitive price for the average Filipino farmer. Consequently, the water buffalo remains the main beast of burden.

As a result of continued poverty and poor sanitation, many Filipinos suffer from malnutrition and disease. Tuberculosis, a major killer in rural areas, could probably be stamped out if medicines and nutritious foods were more widely and readily available.

What the People Eat

Farm families raise almost all their own food. Few people buy much at the store other than salt. In addition to garden vegetables, a family may also raise chickens, but these, too, are considered something of a luxury and are frequently sold at the market. Nevertheless, chickens are a major source of protein. The village dogs, which are considered a great delicacy, are also eaten on special occasions.

But meat, fish, and poultry are generally served only a few times a week and then only in small portions. All three daily meals are much the same and consist of rice, vegetables, and perhaps a piece of fruit—papaya, banana, or coconut. Occasionally, there are butter and eggs. Usually, there is a bunlike bread called *pan de sal.*

Education
and Recreation

Education in the Philippines is compulsory through the sixth grade. But only about half of the Filipino children who enter first grade finish the sixth. This is because funds provided by the Marcos government are insufficient to supply free textbooks and other study materials as well as free lunches. Many elementary school children also drop out of school to help out on the family farm. School is where many Filipinos learn to speak English, because from the third grade on, English is the language of instruction.

Four-year secondary schools are largely privately financed, although there is some government funding. There are more than forty colleges and universities in the Philippines. But most of these are private, although the University of the Philippines is public. Several teachers colleges turn out more than enough teachers for the inadequate public school system. About a quarter of all secondary school graduates go on to college.

Recreation is extremely limited, consisting mainly of dances and local fiestas. Movies are found only in the cities. Spectator sports include baseball, soccer, basketball, boxing, and cockfighting, which is second only to jai alai in popularity. Jai alai is somewhat like handball, with the players using a basketlike scoop to catch and hurl the ball back against the court wall.

Home entertainment consists mainly of listening to the radio. Small transistor radios are highly prized; almost no farm families have television sets. Occasionally, some enterprising storekeeper in the village will buy a TV set to increase business in his or her establishment. Newspapers are popular and sell for only a few centavos. In the pre-Marcos period, freeedom of the press was practiced. Today, the media are rigidly controlled and censored by the government.

Filipino Youth

With the general poverty and lack of opportunity in the villages, more and more young people in recent years have been leaving their homes. Their usual destination is the city, such as Manila, but many also go abroad.

The life they find in the cities, however, is hardly an improvement. In Manila, they often live in the slums along with a third of the rest of the city's population. Houses there are shanties made of flattened tin cans, cardboard, and scrap lumber. Life in the slums is also lonely and dangerous. To get out of this environment, it is necessary to obtain a high-paying job, but such jobs are few and far between.

A surprising number of people with college degrees live in the shantytowns. This is because jobs for professionals such as teachers, engineers, and scientists are hard to find and low paying. Literally thousands of degree-holding young people work in Manila for the equivalent of $100 a month or even less as store clerks, maids, or servants.

Many of these frustrated youths eventually decide to leave the Philippines entirely and take their chances abroad. This is encouraged by the Marcos government. Every young person who leaves the Philippines reduces the pressure on the domestic job market. In addition, the country obtains valuable foreign currency through the money that is sent home from young people overseas to their families. In 1983, some three-quarters of a million Filipinos working abroad sent $1 billion home to their families.

UNREST AT HOME

Obviously, such conditions of general poverty blight the daily lives of the people, both young and old, who continue to live in the Philippines. And this gloomy atmosphere breeds widespread political turmoil. Because the Marcos government seems unable to improve the situation, the average Filipino has begun to turn to local revolutionary groups for more dramatic remedial action.

One of these groups is a kind of grass-roots guerrilla organization called the New People's Army, or NPA. The NPA is inclined to go its own way, ignoring local police and national army efforts to stamp out oppression and corruption. NPA leaders, in fact, regard the police and the military as part of the Philippines' problem of oppression, since it is their guns that keep the dictatorial Marcos government in power. On several occasions, small military detachments in remote rural areas have been ambushed and slain by NPA guerrillas.

The problem with the NPA, as the United States sees it, is that it is a communist organization, and the United States has long fought the spread of communism throughout the Pacific and in Southeast Asia. Marcos, too, has been a long-time foe of communism. But by declaring martial law, which he said was necessary to stamp out the communists, he soon turned the Philippines into as oppressive a political government as that in any communist country.

Since coming to power, Marcos has tripled the size of the national army, but the red guerrillas have also grown in strength and boldness. They have even become aggressive enough to attack government troops, killing a number of them late in 1982 and early in 1983. At the time of Aquino's death, Marcos claimed to have the NPA under control, but this is doubtful.

WHO ARE THE NPA?

The NPA was originally a movement of college and university intellectuals. Today, it includes college students, workers, and a number of Catholic priests. The body of its guerrilla army, however, is made up of rural young men who are sick and tired of poverty, government corruption and oppression, and a continued lack of opportunity under the Marcos government.

To date, the NPA has soft-pedaled its communist ties. This may be because of the Catholic priests in the organization. The Roman Catholic Church is a stout foe of communism, and since the Philippines is predominantly Catholic, the NPA does not want to emphasize this side of its background too strongly. The announced NPA political line is that it wants to better the life of the poor Filipino people. Of course, this is the traditional party line before communists assume control of a country.

But there is no flat denial on the part of NPA leaders that theirs is a communist organization. What would actually occur if the NPA eventually came to power is not known. If it is indeed communist, greater oppression than ever would doubtless settle on the Philippines, for there are no greater oppressors in the world than true Soviet-style communists.

This, of course, is what the United States as well as the bulk of the Philippine people want to avoid. It is the main reason why the United States has continued to support the anticommunist Marcos government despite its obvious failings and broken promises.

III
___
WHO IS
FERDINAND
MARCOS?

How does a heroic young freedom fighter turn into an aging military despot? That is a question many people have asked about Ferdinand Marcos, sixth president of the Philippines since that country gained its independence from the United States in 1946.

Ferdinand Edralin Marcos was born in Sarrat in northern Luzon on September 11, 1917. His father was Mariano R. Marcos, a well-known lawyer and politician. His mother, Josea Edralin Marcos, was a schoolteacher. He was the oldest of four children.

Young Ferdinand's father was a strict disciplinarian who schooled the boy in athletics and the use of weapons. When Ferdinand was just sixteen, he won the small-bore rifle shooting championship of the Philippines. The elder Marcos also taught his son to be an accomplished speaker in three languages, English, Spanish, and Tagalog.

Until he was eight, young Ferdinand was educated by his mother both at home and in the one-room schoolhouse in Sarrat where she taught. In 1925, the elder Marcos was elected to the Philippine Congress, and the family moved to Manila. Young Marcos completed elementary school and high school there, leading his class scholastically and excelling in sports.

From an early age Ferdinand had a remarkable memory. This stood him in good stead at the University of the Philippines, where books were scarce and available to each student for only short periods of time. His ability to quickly memorize pages in a book won him a scholarship to study law. He passed his bar examinations in 1939 with a score of 98.01. This mark was so high that he was suspected of cheating. In response to these charges, young Marcos insisted that he be reexamined orally, and he passed this test with a score of 92.35.

At this point Ferdinand's meteoric career was brought to an abrupt though temporary halt, when he was belatedly accused of having shot and killed Julio Nalundasan, a political rival of his father's, back in 1935. Nalundasan had been killed by a .22 caliber bullet. Young Marcos was known, of course, to be an expert with the .22, and he was also known to be fanatically loyal to his father. Why the charge against him came so late was not clear, but it was suspected that there was a political motive behind it.

Nevertheless, in the fall of 1939, young Marcos was found guilty of being the trigger-man in the assassination. The case was immediately appealed to the Philippine Supreme Court with Ferdinand himself arguing the appeal. In 1940, the verdict of guilty was reversed, and young Marcos joined his father's Manila law firm.

The trial and the youthful Marcos' successful self-defense brought him national attention. Many Filipinos regarded Ferdinand as a young hero whom political enemies of his father had tried to destroy. Soon Marcos was to become an even greater hero.

THE PHILIPPINES' MOST
DECORATED SOLDIER

The Japanese invaded the Philippines shortly after they attacked Pearl Harbor on December 7, 1941. Since the U.S. Pacific fleet had been all but destroyed in the Pearl Harbor attack, no immediate military assistance could be given to the Philippines. A relative handful of U.S. Regular Army soldiers and their Filipino allies fought on alone against the overwhelming superiority of the Japanese invasion forces. One of the most heroic of the Philippine defenders was Ferdinand Marcos, who was soon to become his country's most decorated soldier.

When the war began in the Pacific, Marcos was an intelligence officer working with the U.S. armed forces to gain secret information about the enemy. Soon, the Americans and their Filipino allies were driven onto the narrow Bataan peninsula, where they set up a last-ditch defense. In the Bataan battle, Marcos was wounded and became one of the hundreds of prisoners captured by the Japanese when Bataan fell. The Japanese then forced these prisoners to go on a 200-mile (320-km) death march from Bataan to Camp O'Donnell in central Luzon. Almost a thousand thirst-crazed, starving Americans and Filipinos died on this march. Despite his wounds, Marcos survived.

Marcos also managed to survive the concentration camp conditions of Camp O'Donnell, where as many as three hundred prisoners died each day. When the Japanese discovered that Marcos had been an intelligence officer, they tortured him for more than a week, but he never gave them any secret information.

When he recovered from this ordeal, Marcos managed to escape and join the Filipino resistance forces. He soon became a guerrilla leader and established an organization known as the "Free Men." The Free Men gathered intelligence information and forwarded it to U.S. General Douglas MacArthur, who had managed to escape from the Philippines and establish headquarters in Australia. MacArthur had vowed to return and was already busy planning his strategy for liberating the Philippines. For his efforts in supplying the American forces with information they needed for their planned return, Marcos was awarded a Silver Star.

He won a second Silver Star when MacArthur and the U.S. forces did indeed return to the Philippines in 1944. By the end of the war, Marcos had been decorated with more than twenty Filipino and American medals, including the Distinguished Service Cross, and had attained the rank of colonel.

POSTWAR ENTRY
INTO POLITICS

After the war, Marcos resumed his law practice and soon came to be regarded as the Philippines' most successful trial lawyer. In 1947, as a member of the Philippines Veterans Commission, he succeeded in having Filipino war veterans accepted under the American G.I. Bill of Rights. This enabled them to get low-interest loans, receive money to go to college, and become eligible for numerous other benefits.

In 1949, Marcos decided to enter politics and thus follow in the footsteps of his father, who had been killed fighting the Japanese. Marcos first ran for the Philippine House of Representatives and won the election by a wide margin. He was reelected in 1953 and 1957.

As a congressman, Marcos introduced legislation reducing taxes on small landowners. He also became House minority leader and was the chairman of several key House committees. His record was so good that for ten straight years the Philippine Congressional Press

Club named him as one of the outstanding congressmen.

In 1959, Marcos ran for the Senate. He won his election by the largest margin in the Republic's history. As a senator, Marcos was a champion of civil liberties, land reform, and the trade union movement. He was also a member of the Philippine delegation to the United Nations several times.

Marcos now had his eye on the presidency. But party leaders insisted that several older members deserved to get the nomination ahead of him. As a result, he left the Liberal party and joined the opposition—the Nationalist party. In 1964, the Nationalists nominated Marcos for president, and on November 9, 1965, he defeated his opponent, Diasdado Macapagal, by more than 650,000 votes. Actually, there was very little difference in the political goals of the two parties, as mentioned earlier. Voter preferences were made more on the basis of personalities than issues.

A PRESIDENT FOR REFORM

During his first term in office, Marcos was truly a president in favor of reform. He reduced waste in government spending by eliminating thousands of patronage jobs. Patronage jobs are jobs controlled by the party in power and awarded to loyal party members. He introduced land reform measures and authorized government subsidies to farmers. These measures took land away from large landowners and sold it to poor farmers at low prices. He fought crime and corruption both inside and outside government. His efforts as a fighter against corruption, however, were hampered by the fact that graft had become so ingrained in Philippine politics that it was regarded by many as an acceptable way of life. For generations people had been paying bribes to

Ferdinand Marcos at his inauguration
ceremonies on December 30, 1965,
wearing a sheer, embroidered tagalag,
the traditional Philippine formal wear.

politicians to obtain jobs, get taxes reduced, keep utilities working, and even to get favorable decisions in civil and criminal court cases.

One opposition group that arose to fight corruption in government was the communist Hukbalahaps, commonly called the Huks. The Huks favored the overthrow of the Philippine democratic government and wanted to replace it with a Marxist-Leninist communist regime. Marcos was fanatically opposed to the Huks— just as he later opposed the New People's Army—and in this he was staunchly backed by several U.S. presidential administrations.

Soon the United States was providing huge loans to help improve economic conditions in the Philippines and supporting Marcos in his efforts to stamp out the communists. He did this by declaring communist activity illegal and throwing active communists in jail. These efforts gradually all but abolished the Philippines' democratic government, and Marcos took over as a military dictator. But he did not do so without opposition. One of those who stoutly opposed him was Benigno Aquino.

BENIGNO AQUINO
COMES ON THE SCENE

Benigno "Ninoy" Aquino had not fought in World War II. He was too young. But he did become a political hero to his people. Born in 1932 in Concepcion, north of Manila, Aquino was a member of a prominent family of politicians and plantation owners. Like Marcos, he became a lawyer-politician.

A political prodigy, Aquino had been elected mayor of his hometown of Concepcion when he was just twenty-two, and governor of his province, Tarlac, at the age of twenty-eight. When he was thirty-four, he was elected to the Philippine Senate and almost immediately became a political rival of Marcos. Aquino believed that

Marcos was a dictator who had to be overthrown if human rights and civil liberties were to be restored.

Although Marcos had been elected president by a wide margin in 1965, Aquino's Liberal party staged a comeback and made a strong showing in the senatorial elections of 1971. According to public opinion polls, Aquino and his Liberals were strongly favored to regain control of the government in the next election, scheduled for 1973. Aquino himself would be running as the Liberal party's presidential candidate.

By a curious quirk of political fortune, however, Aquino would not be running against Marcos himself but rather Marcos' wife, Imelda. Since the Philippines was still operating under its old constitution, Marcos was not eligible to run for a third term, so it was expected that he would have his wife stand in for him.

It was at this point, in 1972, that Marcos confounded everybody by declaring martial law and having Aquino jailed. Aquino was charged with murder, subversive activity, and illegal possession of firearms. No evidence was presented to support these charges, however. Aquino was kept in jail at Fort Bonifacio near Manila until 1977, when he was finally convicted of all charges against him and sentenced to death. But his execution was delayed because of American objections to the Marcos regime's continued violations of human and civil rights, In 1980, Aquino was released on the condition that he go to the U.S. for corrective heart surgery.

In the United States, Aquino successfully underwent a heart bypass operation in Dallas. When he recovered, he obtained research fellowships at Harvard and the Massachusetts Institute of Technology. But his mended heart was still in the Philippines. He could not return there, however, for fear of once again being thrown into jail. In the end, his patriotism and his growing opposition to the Marcos government made him decide to risk returning to his homeland.

In 1983, when Aquino decided to return to the Philippines, President Marcos sent his wife, Imelda, to New York to try to persuade Aquino to change his mind. By now, the exiled Aquino had become a popular hero to the Filipinos, and Marcos feared that his return would result in antigovernment demonstrations. In a lengthy meeting at the Philippines consulate in New York, Imelda relayed her husband's warning about the threat to Aquino's life and told him, "Think of your family for a change. You can all remain in New York and enjoy life." Aquino told friends that through Imelda Marcos he had been offered any amount of money he wanted to support himself, his wife Corazon, and their family of five children as long as he stayed in the United States.

Not only did Aquino refuse the offer, but he calmly accepted the threat to his life and returned to the Philippines prepared, if necessary, to die. Comparing himself to another, earlier Filipino martyr, José B. Rizal, who returned from exile in 1892 only to eventually be executed by the Spanish, Aquino told reporters who accompanied him on the plane to his homeland, "If I should die at the hand of the oppressors, let it be."

IMELDA MARCOS,
THE "IRON BUTTERFLY"

Imelda Marcos is one of the most interesting and powerful women in Philippine history. As ambitious and ruthless a politician as her husband, Imelda Marcos is known to many Filipinos as the "Iron Butterfly."

Ferdinand Marcos and Imelda Romualdez of Tacloban, Leyte, were married in 1954. The Romualdez family was one of the wealthiest and most influential families in the Philippines. Among her relatives were judges, governors, and provincial administrators who controlled more than half a million votes in the central part of the Republic.

Imelda had little formal education, but she had strong political interests. She was also a great beauty, and as the "Rose of Tacloban" (after her hometown) was named Miss Manila the same year she and the dashing young congressman, Ferdinand Marcos, were married. She is thirteen years younger than her husband.

From the very beginning of their marriage, Imelda Marcos proved to be a big help to her husband's political career. During his campaigns for the senate and the presidency, she accompanied him, making emotional speeches and singing songs to entertain the voters. Aquino once observed that the Iron Butterfly was worth a million votes to her husband.

There are three Marcos children, a son, Ferdinand, Jr., and two daughters, Maria Imelda, and Maria Victoria.

At first, Imelda Marcos claimed she had no political ambitions of her own, but soon after her husband declared martial law this attitude began to change. Marcos named her governor of metropolitan Manila and appointed her to the fifteen-member executive committee. This powerful panel advises Marcos on all government decisions and has the right to decide who will succeed him should he die in office or simply resign. She has denied any desire to succeed her husband as president, and in late 1983 she resigned from this post. But despite her denials she has remained a prime candidate for the office and still holds the powerful position of Minister of Human Settlement.

Marcos swearing in his wife, Imelda, as the governor of Manila in 1975. Mrs. Marcos resigned from this post— one of the most powerful in the government— in 1983, but her political ambitions remain high.

Many opponents of the Marcos government fear Imelda Marcos as much as they fear her husband and would stoutly oppose her taking over as president. She has been ruthless in weeding out enemies of her husband's regime and has spent enormous sums of money for her pet projects. These have included redecorating the Malacañang Palace, the presidential residence; the construction of a $10-million films festival center; and the building of a small palace made entirely of coconuts that was intended to attract the tourist trade.

Another of Imelda Marcos' projects was intended to soften the criticism of her husband's failure to improve the Philippine economy. This project, called the National Livelihood Movement, made available $500 million in low-interest loans to small businessmen and farmers. In a society where the average income is about $12 a week, this money was more than welcome. But so much of it was drained off in graft and corruption that the lot of the poor businessmen and farmers was unchanged.

Charges of corruption have always met with sharp, unsatisfactory responses from the Philippines' First Lady. When asked how she and her husband had become so wealthy—estimates say the First Family is now worth more than $1.5 billion—Imelda replied, "Some people are just smarter than others."

ATTEMPT ON THE
IRON BUTTERFLY'S LIFE

According to the former information secretary of the Philippines, Francisco S. Tatad, at least eight attempts have been made on the lives of President Marcos and his wife. The most serious and most nearly successful attempt took place on December 7, 1972, when Imelda Marcos narrowly escaped assassination.

The attack took place at Pasay City near Manila, where Mrs. Marcos was presenting awards to winners in a national beautification and cleanliness contest. During the ceremony, a man wielding a long knife slashed Mrs. Marcos on her hands and arms. The attacker, later identified as Carlito Dimailig, twenty-seven, was immediately shot and killed by bodyguards. Mrs. Marcos was rushed to a Manila hospital, where seventy-five stitches were required to close her wounds.

Although the would-be assassin had no known political connection, Information Secretary Tatad said Dimailig was widely known for his bitter opposition to President Marcos and had chosen Imelda Marcos as a target for his wrath. Following the attempt on Mrs. Marcos' life, some eighty-five persons, including several prominent Filipino citizens, were detained for questioning, but it was finally decided that Dimailig had acted on his own.

IMELDA'S WASTEFUL WAYS
STILL AN IRRITANT

In the poverty-stricken Philippines, the Iron Butterfly's flamboyant and extravagant life style continues to anger many of her countrymen and -women. When President and Mrs. Marcos came to the United States on an official visit in 1982, they arrived with three hundred suitcases and forty aides. Imelda is also known for her wild shopping sprees in the United States and Europe. Once she went so far as to buy a jet airplane for the family's use, but it had to be kept in a hangar in Hawaii because her husband feared the reaction from his poor Filipino followers.

If the Marcos regime is overthrown, and the Iron Butterfly and her husband have to flee the Philippines, their refuge is already available for them. It is in the United States on a 50-acre estate on Long Island near New York City. President and Imelda Marcos recently bought this estate for $1 million.

In order to fully understand the modern history of the Philippines, it is important to know something about the early days of the Philippines' long fight for freedom and democracy. The members of the Marcos regime are not the first oppressors with whom the freedom-loving Filipinos have had to do battle.

IV

EARLY
HISTORY OF
THE
PHILIPPINES

Probably the first people to occupy the Philippines were the Negritos, some 25,000 years ago. It is not known for sure where they came from. The Negritos were followed by Indonesians and Malays from the East Indies. This was several hundred years before the birth of Christ. During the next several centuries, trade developed between the Philippines and China, and many Chinese also later settled on the islands. Still later, Moslem Arab missionaries arrived and converted the Moros of Mindanao Island to Islam, the Moslem religion. The whole of the Philippines might today be an Arab or Oriental nation had it not been for the arrival of the Spanish in the sixteenth century.

In 1521, explorer Ferdinand Magellan on his round-the-world voyage anchored the Spanish fleet in Cebu harbor. Magellan and his men became friendly with the people of Cebu Island and aided them in an invasion of neighboring Mactan Island. Magellan was killed in this action, but the rest of his crew later went on to complete the historic first voyage around the world. Also, at a later time, the Philippines were named after King Philip II of Spain.

Magellan's first contact with the Philippines was soon followed by several Spanish colonizing expeditions. The Spanish were seeking rare spices and attempting to expand their empire into Southeast Asia. These colonizing expeditions brought with them many Spanish priests and friars, who set about converting the Filipinos, whom they called "Indios," to Roman Catholicism. Few rare spices were found in the Philippines, but the islands were a fertile field for religious conversions. Even many of the Chinese merchants there were converted to Roman Catholicism.

Many of these converted Chinese married Filipino women, and there were numerous other racially mixed marriages. Their descendants were known as *mestizos,* or people of mixed blood. When the Spanish took control of the islands, the mestizos became a wealthy merchant and plantation-owning class who sent their children abroad to school. These well-educated youths came to be called *ilustrados,* or enlightened ones, and when they returned to their homeland they began to demand social change and more of a say in the government of the Philippines. These were the first signs of nationalism and a desire for independence among the Filipinos.

JOSÉ RIZAL, FIRST FILIPINO MARTYR

While studying in Europe in the late nineteenth century, a group of young ilustrados formed a Philippine independence organization. The first leader of this group, which was called simply the "Propaganda Movement," was a young intellectual named José B. Rizal. Rizal came to believe that a revolution was needed to gain independence for the Philippines.

Rizal and the other members of the Propaganda Movement were beaten to the punch, however, by a young revolutionary back in the Philippines named Andrés Bonifacio. Bonifacio was not an ilustrado. In fact, he had very little education. He worked as a clerk in a store in Manila. But within him the fires of freedom burned brightly.

Bonifacio organized a secret revolutionary society named *Katipunan*, or "Sons of the People." Unsupported by the ilustrados, Bonifacio led his young revolutionaries in a rebellion against the Spanish authorities in San Juan del Monte province in the summer of 1896. Meanwhile, Rizal had returned to the Philippines, where news of his own revolutionary intentions preceded his arrival. Though neither Rizal nor any other ilustrado backed the Katipunan movement, Rizal was seized and thrown in jail when the Katipunan rebellion broke out.

Rizal was held in jail until the end of the year. Then, on December 30, 1896, he was executed by a firing squad.

Rizal's execution caused the Katipunan and ilustrado forces to unite. But a power struggle then began between Bonifacio and a rising young military leader named Emilio Aguinaldo. Bonifacio was killed in the struggle, and Aguinaldo emerged as the undisputed leader of the Filipino revolutionary forces.

These revolutionary forces, however, had been badly weakened in their fight with one another. The Spanish took advantage of this situation by offering to grant amnesty to the revolutionaries and pay Aguinaldo and some of his followers a large sum of money if he would voluntarily go into exile. They also promised certain political reforms that were never actually put into practice. Aguinaldo accepted this offer late in 1897, and he and his aides left for Hong Kong, where they awaited a favorable opportunity to return to the Philippines.

THE SPANISH-AMERICAN
WAR: ENTER
THE UNITED STATES

In the spring of 1898, the United States and Spain went to war. The dispute was over Cuba. Years of Spanish misrule of that island had caused the Cubans to rebel against Spain in 1895. The United States sympathized with the rebels, and there was much talk—especially in the American press—about the United States intervening in the revolution.

Earlier, the United States had tried to buy Cuba from Spain. When this offer was refused, American efforts to set Cuba free continued. The Cuban revolution seemed like an ideal chance to force the Spanish to grant Cuba its independence. While considering armed intervention in the conflict, the United States sent the battleship *Maine* into Cuba's Havana harbor.

On the night of February 15, 1898, the *Maine* blew up, killing 260 American sailors. To this day, it is not known who or what caused the explosion, but the American press accused Spain of the act. "Remember the Maine!" soon became a nationwide battlecry, and on April 25, 1898, war was declared by the United States against Spain.

WAR BEGINS IN
THE PHILIPPINES

The first battle of the Spanish-American War did not take place in Cuba, however, but in the far-off Philippines. Certain that with the sinking of the *Maine* war with Spain was imminent, Assistant Secretary of the Navy Theodore Roosevelt had placed Commodore George Dewey in command of the U.S. Asiatic fleet and told him to prepare the fleet for action in the Philippines. According to legend, when told of Roosevelt's orders, President William McKinley commented that he knew that Spain owned the Philippines but confessed he wasn't sure where they were.

A week after the United States declared war on Spain, McKinley knew where the Philippines were. In fact, the whole world knew, for they were the scene of one of the most decisive, one-sided naval battles in the history of sea warfare.

Early on the Sunday morning of May 1, 1898, Commodore Dewey's U.S. Asiatic fleet steamed into Manila Bay, where a large part of the Spanish Pacific war fleet was stationed. When the Spanish ships came within range, Dewey told the captain of the flagship *Olympia*, "You may fire when ready, Gridley."

A few hours later, ten of the Spanish major warships were sunk and several hundred Spanish sailors were dead. No American ships were badly damaged, and no American lives were lost.

With this action, the United States began to play an important role in the history of the Philippines.

THE RETURN OF
EMILIO AGUINALDO

When he learned of the defeat of the Spanish war fleet in Manila Bay, the exiled revolutionary Emilio Aguinaldo immediately returned to the Philippines to lead a revolution against Spain. The Filipinos heralded Aguinaldo's return and rallied to his side. Independence seemed to be at hand. Aguinaldo, of course, having received arms from the U.S. government, expected full support from the United States in his and his people's declaration of independence. In this he was to be severely disappointed.

Soon after President McKinley learned the location of the Philippine Islands, he began to realize their stra-

*The arrival of the U.S. Asiatic fleet
in Manila Bay at the start of
the Spanish-American War marked the
beginning of U.S. involvement in the Philippines.*

tegic importance. Control of them would make the United States both a major power in the Pacific and a world power. Although there was some loud public opposition to the United States becoming an imperialist nation, McKinley and other government officials began to make plans to take over, or annex, the Philippines. When he got wind of these plans, Aguinaldo prepared to fight the United States.

The Spanish-American War was a short conflict and ended in complete victory for the United States. The Philippines thus became the first and only colony the United States ever had. In Cuba, the first American troops landed on the coast in June of 1898, and the last fighting occurred with the Spanish surrender of Santiago on July 17. Spain agreed to an armistice on August 12. Formal fighting in the Philippines ended a few days later, and a peace treaty was signed in Paris on December 10, 1898. Spain granted Cuba its independence and ceded the Philippines to the United States. In return for the Philippines, the U.S. paid Spain $20 million.

THE PHILIPPINE INSURRECTION

Aguinaldo and his Filipino followers refused to accept U.S. control of the Philippines. They bitterly resented their country's having been "bought" for a few million dollars, and they were determined to continue their fight for freedom. On January 23, 1899, in the town of Malolos, a national constitution was proclaimed, and Aguinaldo was elected president of the new Republic of the Philippines.

The United States government regarded this establishment of a separate government as unlawful. President McKinley called it an insurrection—somewhat as if an American state had defied the federal government—

and labeled Aguinaldo and his followers insurrectionists, or *insurrectos*. The president ordered General Elwell
S. Otis and his U.S. Army troops who were still in Manila following the Spanish surrender to capture or kill
Aguinaldo and put down the insurrection.

At Malolos, which was about 30 miles (48 km) from
Manila, Aguinaldo had between thirty thousand and fif-
ty thousand insurrecto troops. The American forces in
Manila numbered only about twelve thousand or four-
teen thousand. But the insurrectos were poorly armed
and lacked ammunition for the few guns they had.
Many Filipinos were armed only with spears or
machete-like bolo knives.

Aguinaldo and his insurrectos had one major advantage. Many of them were stationed in blockhouses surrounding Manila. The major U.S. advantage was its
naval warships stationed in Manila harbor, against
which the Filipinos had no defense. Most of the fighting
during the insurrection took place on the island of
Luzon.

THE FIGHTING BEGINS

Fighting began on February 4, 1899, when the insurrectos attacked Manila. The Americans fought back fiercely
and on the following day launched a counterattack. One
of the two U.S. divisions that took part in this counterattack was led by General Arthur MacArthur, father of
World War II hero Douglas MacArthur.

The American forces were supported by artillery,
Gatling guns—forerunner of the machine gun—and
ships' guns from the U.S. Navy. The fighting lasted for
two days, and when it was over the insurrecto forces
were shattered and in full retreat. They had suffered
more than 3,000 casualties, the United States about 250.
General Otis prepared to inform Washington that the
insurrection had been put down and that the fight for
the Philippines had ended. Otis did not send the mes-

sage, however, because he and his men soon realized that the fight had just started.

The insurrectos now engaged the American troops in guerrilla-style warfare. The roadless, tropical, heavily forested Philippines—like Vietnam some sixty years later—was ideal for guerrilla fighting. It was impossible for the Americans to mount a major offensive against small bands of Filipinos who struck secretly, often by night, or set up ambushes during the day along jungle trails, attacked silently, and then faded into the tropical forests. Artillery and naval guns were useless against such furtive attackers. The heavy Gatling guns could not be hauled through the thick forest undergrowth.

General Otis had been trained in traditional warfare, and he continued to try orthodox methods of fighting the guerrillas. During the next seven months, an additional thirty-five thousand U.S. troops arrived in the Philippines, and Otis continued to waste them in futile attacks on an enemy that refused to fight in open battle. The Filipinos—again as the Vietcong guerrillas would later do in Vietnam—stealthily cut the Americans down by eating away at their flanks, killing a handful of men here, another handful there, with silent, murderous swings of their bolo knives, or by dropping them a man at a time with spears hurled from out of nowhere. Morale among the Americans began to deteriorate as casualties mounted and the fighting seemed to go on both endlessly and futilely.

Nevertheless, with its enormously superior manpower and firepower, General MacArthur's division was able to capture Aguinaldo's headquarters at Malolos. But Aguinaldo had already fled and was rallying his scattered forces elsewhere in the jungle. A victory without the capture of Aguinaldo was an empty one, so the guerrilla warfare continued. To make matters worse, soon the rainy season had set in, and it was impossible for the United States to even attempt to resume any full-scale fighting until the autumn of 1899.

PRESIDENT MCKINLEY
TAKES A HAND

Among the U.S. military forces in the Philippines were a few officers and enlisted men to whom guerrilla warfare was somewhat familiar. These were the soldiers who had fought the American Indians in the West and Southwest. They had learned that success in guerrilla warfare depended on speed, daring, cunning, surprise, and perhaps most important, attacking the enemy with small, highly mobile bodies of men.

One of these officers who had become highly skilled in frontier fighting against the Indians was a small, wiry, red-haired colonel named Frederick Funston. Funston now determined to use his own guerrilla skills and those of a handful of his Twentieth Regiment of Kansas volunteers to capture Aguinaldo. But Funston could not get permission from General Otis to lead a small raiding party into insurrecto territory.

General Otis was still determined to defeat the insurrectos in open battle, and when the dry season began in October of 1899, he resumed his full-scale assault. During the next year, several hundred separate engagements were fought, but at the end of this time the insurrectos seemed to be as strong and as invincible as ever.

At this point President McKinley decided to take a hand in solving the problem. He appointed a civil governor to try to bring order out of the chaos of the Philippines. The man he appointed was William Howard Taft, a future U.S. president.

Taft was as able a man as he was big—he weighed some 300 pounds (135 kg)—and when he arrived in the Philippines in the spring of 1900 he immediately went to work. General Otis' resignation was accepted, and General MacArthur was named to replace him. While MacArthur formulated military plans to subdue the insurrectionists, Taft went about his business devising civil plans to subdue them. Schools were built, villages were restored, medical aid was made available, and a modest form of self-government was established among the civilian population. To receive these benefits, however, the Filipinos had to take an oath of allegiance to the United States. Most were happy to do so, although a large body of insurrectos still remained at large and fought any attempts to establish a civil government. Taft and MacArthur both knew that the American efforts could never be wholly successful as long as Aguinaldo remained at large.

THE CAPTURE OF AGUINALDO

Early in 1901, Funston—a general officer now—presented his raiding party plan to General MacArthur. MacArthur immediately approved it. A few days later, Funston's men captured an insurrecto messenger named Cecilio Segismundo and persuaded him to tell them where Aguinaldo's headquarters were now located. Segismundo, who was weary of the war, told them Aguinaldo was in a village named Palanan in northeastern Luzon. He also agreed to lead them there. Funston then devised an ingenious plan to capture Aguinaldo.

Segismundo, it turned out, was not the only insurrecto who was war-weary. Many insurrectos, Segismundo said, wanted to surrender to the Americans, but they were fearful of being killed if they did so. Funston told Segismundo to get together a party of these defecting insurrectos and bring them to U.S. headquarters. When this was done, Funston made up a story that he hoped Aguinaldo would believe. Funston told Segismundo to notify Aguinaldo that some insurrecto troops had captured five American officers and that Segismundo and the insurrectos were bringing them to Aguinaldo's headquarters. Aguinaldo's reply indicated that he would be delighted to receive such important prisoners.

Funston and four of his hand-picked officers, pretending to be prisoners, then set out for Palanan accompanied by Segismundo and the band of insurrecto defectors acting as their "guards." The party left Manila on February 11, 1901.

The trip to Palanan was the most difficult part of the capture of Aguinaldo. It took Funston, his men, and their "guards" almost two months to complete the journey through some of the most rugged jungle country in the Philippines.

Once they arrived, however, there was only a brief struggle with Aguinaldo's guards before the mission was accomplished. During the struggle, Funston's men wanted to kill Aguinaldo, but Funston threw himself on top of the rebel leader to protect him and ordered his men to hold their fire. A few weeks later, Aguinaldo was returned to Manila.

The capture of Aguinaldo broke the back of the insurrection, although small bands of insurrectos carried on the fighting for many months. Ironically, Aguinaldo was only in captivity a short time before he gave his oath of allegiance to the United States.

The Philippine insurrection did not formally end until July 4, 1902. On that date a proclamation that hostilities had ceased was signed by a new U.S. president. Since the new president had been a key person in starting hostilities against the Philippines, it was perhaps fitting that he should officially end them. His name was Theodore Roosevelt.

Captured insurrection leader Emilio Aguinaldo on a United States gunboat in 1901

V

MODERN HISTORY OF THE PHILIPPINES

Soon after the United States gained complete control of the Philippines, it began to make plans for their independence as a republic. Unfortunately, these plans took almost half a century to be implemented. This was because there were many American government officials who believed that the "little brown brother," as the Philippine people were condescendingly called, had to grow up and prepare themselves for independence.

In the interim, the United States governed the islands through a five-man commission headed by a civil governor, William Howard Taft. The commission gave many responsible island government jobs to the ilustrados. Many additional Filipinos also gained authority in the national legislature or assembly, which was established in 1907. In 1916, the commission was replaced by an elected House and Senate. Finally, in 1934, the U.S. Congress passed the Tydings-McDuffie Act, which said that the Philippines would be given complete independence after ten years of successful self-government.

The following year, 1935, the Commonwealth of the Philippines was established, and Manual L. Quezon was elected its first president. During World War II, when the Japanese took over the Philippines, Quezon formed a government in exile in Washington, D.C. He died in 1944 and was succeeded by Sergio Osmena. Quezon City, just northeast of Manila, was named in honor of Quezon and served temporarily as the nation's capital.

THE JAPANESE
OCCUPATION OF
THE PHILIPPINES

The Philippines suffered severely at the hands of the Japanese during World War II. When they first took over the islands in January of 1942, the Japanese made a show of being friendly toward the Filipinos. They played up the fact that they were all Oriental brothers and sisters who should be opposed to the white imperialistic Americans. Of course, having the Filipinos on their side would have helped the Japanese in fighting the war. A friendly Philippines would have eliminated the need for stationing large forces of occupation troops there.

To prove their good intentions, the Japanese freed many of the Filipino troops who had fought against them on Bataan and encouraged them to take up arms against the Americans. Few did so. They, as well as most other Filipinos, were skeptical of these gestures of friendship. But a small number of civilians readily accepted them and began to collaborate with the enemy. Many of these collaborators were well-to-do Filipinos who hoped to curry favor with the Japanese and thus gain additional food and other privileges. This situation would eventually cause a radical split in postwar Philippine society.

Meanwhile, the Japanese shrewdly took advantage of the Filipino nationalistic desire for independence by declaring the Philippines an independent republic in 1943. This move won additional converts. But the Filipino skeptics pointed out that the so-called "independent republic" was a sham. The new government had not been elected, and the new president, José P. Laurel, was a collaborator chosen for the job by the Japanese military authorities.

It was not long before the Japanese occupation forces showed their true colors. Press censorship was absolute, listening to foreign radio broadcasts was forbidden under penalty of death, failure to cooperate with the Japanese military government also became a capital crime, and valueless money was forced on the civilian populace. When the conquerors confiscated all available rice, a famine on Luzon resulted.

Japanese army troops were especially brutal in their treatment of Filipino civilians, but their crimes of rape and looting went unpunished by the occupation authorities. Soon, Filipino civilians began to take matters into their own hands, ambushing Japanese soldiers by night and killing them. Reprisals were swift and murderous, with some villages being entirely wiped out. Such actions only fanned the flames of Filipino desire to free themselves from their Japanese oppressors. Soon, guerrilla bands were formed—among them the Free Men in which Marcos was active—and the Japanese found themselves engaged in costly guerrilla warfare.

Guerrillas Loyal to MacArthur

One of the main problems the guerrillas had was a lack of weapons. At first, less than a quarter of them were armed with guns. Ammunition had to be severely rationed, with only a few rounds going to each man. Food was scarce. But the guerrillas held one solid advantage over the enemy. That was in their thorough knowledge of the countryside. They could disappear into the jungle or mountains and remain hidden for weeks and months, appearing only occasionally to attack a small party of Japanese. Often these attacks were waged by night, the guerrillas wielding their ancient bolo knives with the same deadly efficiency that their fathers and grandfathers had displayed during the Spanish-American War. Only this time, they were fighting on the side of the Americans.

American friendship had come to mean a great deal to many Filipinos. The Americans had proved themselves to be loyal and fair administrators of the Philippines, even if they had not granted the island republic its independence as soon as many would have liked.

One radical nationalist, Tomas Confesor, went so far as to say, "We have been living during the last forty years under a regime of justice and liberty."

The physical embodiment and living symbol of America's just treatment was Douglas MacArthur, son of General Arthur MacArthur. After the Spanish-American War, Arthur MacArthur had helped to administer the Philippines, and he had bred into his son, Douglas, a love of the Filipinos and a respect for their institutions.

Douglas MacArthur, also like his father, was a graduate of West Point. His first assignment after graduation in 1903 was in the Philippines. Eventually, he would serve four "hitches," or tours of duty, there and come to regard the Philippines as an American trust to be administered fairly and with justice and respect.

Early in his tour of duty in the Philippines, MacArthur became friends with Manuel Quezon, former guerrilla and future president, but that friendship was interrupted by the Japanese invasion. Quezon fled to the United States and MacArthur to Australia, but both men vowed to return. Only death would prevent Quezon from fulfilling his vow; nothing would stop MacArthur.

When he left the Philippines for Australia, MacArthur solemnly stated, "I shall return!" This declaration instantly became a famous wartime battlecry not only in the Philippines but also in the United States. Filipinos universally believed that the United States and MacArthur would live up to the general's word. Vicente Raval, a guerrilla leader and aide to Marcos, later said: "We had total faith in the American promise to come back. We never faltered in our hope."

Aid from MacArthur

When MacArthur left the Philippines, he was not aware of the resistance activity there. But after many weeks, Marcos and his Free Men managed to piece together a shortwave radio and began to broadcast an appeal for aid to MacArthur in Australia. Almost immediately MacArthur began to dispatch arms, ammunition, and other supplies by submarine to the Philippines. At first, these supplies were limited, but within a few months several of the U.S. Navy's largest submarines were making deliveries to the guerrillas of up to 50 tons per trip. Soon, the guerrilla cause began to look brighter.

As the guerrillas became better able to carry on their harassment of the enemy, their ranks swelled. By war's end, they would number some 250,000 and be supported by almost the entire civilian population of the Philippines.

A surprising number of the new guerrilla recruits were American. These men were members of the U.S. armed forces who had escaped from Bataan. They fled into the mountains and jungles and somehow managed to survive until they could make their first contact with friendly Filipino allies. Several of these Americans proved to be outstanding guerrilla leaders.

If MacArthur and his forces were to successfully reinvade the Philippines, what the general needed was specific information on Japanese troop locations and troop and ship movements. To obtain this intelligence information, it was essential that the guerrillas establish observation posts and coast-watcher stations. Then, of course, the information had to be coded and transmitted by radio to Australia.

Getting radios to the guerrillas became a top priority, and when the radios began to arrive in the Philippines, the Americans among the guerrillas were put in charge of encoding the messages. Within a matter of months, a regular transmission network had been set up throughout the islands, and several thousand reports were being sent to MacArthur each month.

Ferdinand Marcos and his Free Men played a key role in gathering intelligence for transmission over this radio network. Marcos had begun working in the Manila underground resistance and had rapidly become famous for his courageous and daring exploits. To avoid detection by the Japanese, he had faked his own death soon after the enemy occupation and even had a false death certificate placed in the Manila city records. One of his aides went even further and had a tombstone with his name on it placed in a prominent place in a local cemetery. For much of the war, among members of his immediate family, only Marcos' mother knew that Ferdinand was alive.

Having been among the first of the guerrillas to establish radio contact with MacArthur, Marcos continued to work closely with the general's headquarters throughout the war. When MacArthur asked the guerrillas to cut back on their ambushing activities against the Japanese and concentrate instead on gathering military intelligence, it was Marcos who put the general's wishes into effect. Many guerrillas preferred killing Japanese to manning isolated coast-watcher stations and reporting on Japanese ship movements, but Marcos saw to it that they obeyed orders.

MacArthur was also concerned that as the strength of the guerrilla forces grew, they might decide to take matters into their own hands and engage the Japanese occupation troops in open battle. This, MacArthur knew, would be suicidal. What he wanted was for the guerrillas to lie low until the United States actually invaded the Philippines and to then stage an uprising. Marcos was instrumental in the accomplishment of this difficult task as well.

Actually, there was considerable danger involved in manning lonely observation posts or coast-watcher stations. As this activity grew, and radio traffic grew with it, the Japanese became fully aware of what was going on. They also became increasingly efficient in combating it. Radio direction finders were used to pinpoint secret radios, with Japanese troops then being sent in to destroy the sending stations and their occupants. Many guerrillas and several important guerrilla leaders were killed in this fashion. But the intelligence effort never ceased. Operators moved about frequently, never transmitting from the same place twice, and whenever operators were apprehended and killed, new volunteers stepped forward to take their place.

MacArthur's Return to the Philippines

In the autumn of 1944, U.S. warplanes taking off from aircraft carriers lying just off the coast began a preinvasion "softening up" of the Philippines. These bombers paved the way for MacArthur's long-heralded return, and the Filipino guerrillas were delighted to see that their intelligence-gathering efforts were at long last paying off. Straight as arrows, the American bombers headed toward Japanese targets identified by the underground guerrillas. Camouflaged ammunition and supply dumps, airfields hidden away in the jungles, Japanese headquarters and communications buildings disguised as civilian dwelling places—all were blasted by the relentless attackers.

It was expected that MacArthur would first come ashore at Mindanao. Instead, he chose Leyte, where American forces began landing in strength on October 20, 1944. MacArthur remained aboard the cruiser *Nashville* while Sixth Army troops made an early morning amphibious landing. When the troops had advanced inland a few thousand feet, MacArthur and his aides boarded a landing craft and headed toward shore. Some 35 yards (32 m) offshore, the landing craft went aground, and MacArthur and his party had to get out and walk. The water was only up to their knees, and a photographer recorded the event in one of the war's most memorable pictures.

After the war, General MacArthur said: "It took me only thirty or forty long strides to reach dry land, but that was one of the most meaningful walks I ever took."

A short time later, MacArthur broadcast his return over the nation's radio network, calling on citizens and guerrillas alike to "rise and strike" the Japanese oppressors. This they did, and with their aid the U.S. infantry, supported by fighter and bomber aircraft, swept way all enemy forces before them. The war, of course, would not end for almost another full year, but the United States and General MacArthur had kept their faith with the Philippine people.

General Douglas MacArthur
with American forces landing
on Leyte Island in 1944

Wartorn Manila after the
Japanese withdrawal in 1944

THE POSTWAR
PHILIPPINES

The United States further lived up to its pledge to the Philippines when it granted that nation its independence on July 4, 1946. Manuel Roxas was elected the first president. Roxas had played an important and risky role during the war. He had remained in Manila posing as a collaborator but secretly passing vital information to Marcos, who relayed it to MacArthur in Australia and Quezon in Washington. When his activities became known after the war, Roxas became a national hero. Unfortunately, he died in 1948, and Elpidio Quirino succeeded him as president. Other Filipinos who had actually collaborated with the Japanese were now accused of disloyalty, but few were actually tried for treason. In fact, many former collaborators went on to gain important positions in the postwar government. This caused great resentment on the part of loyal Filipinos and resulted in a split in society that has not been healed to this day.

During the postwar period, the Philippines had a long and difficult struggle to rebuild from the ravages of war. Manila as well as several other cities had been largely destroyed, and there was a continuing food shortage. The new nation was greatly aided by the United States, which sent $1 billion in economic assistance between 1946 and 1951. Millions of additional dollars were sent over the next three decades.

The Huk Rebellion

The new government of the Philippines was severely hampered during this postwar rebuilding period by the so-called Huks, who tried to overthrow the U.S.-sponsored regime. The communist Huks had a twenty thousand-man army, which tried to seize the government, but after several years of fighting, the Philippine army managed to put down the rebellion—temporarily.

One of the leaders in the fight against the Huks was Ramon Magsaysay. Magsaysay was elected president to succeed Quirino in 1953. Magsaysay was a staunch believer in human rights for all Filipinos—not just the favored rich—and was instrumental in passing important land reform legislation in an attempt to break up the huge plantations in order to help poor farmers. Magsaysay was aided in this reform movement by Benigno Aquino.

Unfortunately, Magsaysay was killed in an airplane crash in the spring of 1957. He was succeeded by Carlos P. Garcia. Garcia was a political moderate, who tried to slow the reform movement and thus appease the protesting large landowners. General dissatisfaction with his efforts led to his being defeated by the Liberal party's candidate, Diosdado Macapagal in 1961. It was Macapagal whom Marcos defeated in 1965 to begin his long, controversial reign as president of the Philippines—a reign that saw the mercurial Marcos mysteriously change from liberal reformer to political despot.

Resumption of the Huk Rebellion Leads to Martial Law

Marcos was scarcely sworn into office before the Huk rebellion was resumed. This time, the Huks were supported by students demanding educational reforms and farmers and workers demanding agriculture and labor reforms.

Since the students, farmers, and laborers were sympathetic to the Huks, Marcos labeled them all communists and insisted that a "Red Revolution" was trying to overthrow the lawful Philippine government and replace it with a Marxist-Leninist socialist regime. This gave Marcos an excuse to declare martial law, which resulted in virtually the complete loss of democratic freedoms, a loss that the Philippines Republic still suffers from today.

VI

THE FUTURE OF THE PHILIPPINES

What does the future hold in store for the troubled island republic of the Philippines?

Investigation into the Benigno Aquino slaying has continued, but by the spring of 1984 the inquiry had raised more questions than it had answered. Military witnesses before the five-member Agrava Commission insisted that communist rebel Rolando Galman was the killer, but several civilian eyewitnesses were equally insistent that he was not.

One civilian witness, named Reuben Regalado, a ground technician who said he inspected the China Airlines plane on which Aquino had arrived in Manila, also said he saw police holding Galman by the arms *before* Aquino was shot.

The four soldiers who had escorted Aquino down the ramp steps promptly sued Regalado for libel, for implying that one of them had done the shooting. But Regalado either left the country or went into hiding immediately after giving his testimony, to avoid any action being taken against him.

Another civilian witness, Ramon Balang, a Philippines Airline ground engineer, said he saw Galman laughing and joking with soldiers near the airplane at the time of the assassination and that Galman was not only unarmed but was also standing some 6 feet (1.8 m) in front of and to the left of Aquino. Official reports and government witnesses had already said that Aquino was shot from behind at point-blank range. Balang said he heard a shot and turned to see Aquino fall. Asked if he thought Galman had shot Aquino, Balang said, "He did not have the opportunity to fire a shot from the position he was in. He was just standing there smiling with his hands empty when there was another volley of gunfire and Galman fell. He did not have a chance to fire a shot."

This testimony, of course, contradicted earlier testimony by other eyewitnesses who said the already lifeless body of Galman was pitched out onto the tarmac from a van after Aquino was killed. Nevertheless, the Balang testimony was so strong that Ernesto Herrera, one of the five civilians appointed by President Marcos to investigate the killing of his chief political rival, said, "It destroys the government version." Herrera added that he hoped Balang's decision to testify would bring other witnesses forward.

Aquino's brother, Agapito, continued to tell reporters that he had eyewitnesses who saw an escort shoot Ninoy. But he never gave their names to the Agrava Commission, claiming that he did not want to see his witnesses killed. He also insisted that there was public distrust of the commission's objectivity and concern for its ties with Marcos. This distrust was expressed in continued anti-Marcos public demonstrations in 1984. In February, more than 500,000 people, many shouting "Revolution!" and "Marcos resign!" jammed the streets of Manila. Riot police were called on to quiet the demonstration.

EFFORTS TO
RESTORE CONFIDENCE
IN GOVERNMENT

Meanwhile, President and Mrs. Marcos acted to strengthen the ruling party's control of the government. First Lady Imelda Marcos announced her resignation from the fifteen-member executive committee, at one time designated to pick a successor to Ferdinand Marcos when it became necessary.

At the same time, President Marcos announced through his political affairs minister, Leonardo Perez, that the position of vice-president would be restored for the next national election. Marcos had earlier abolished this office, thus eliminating any possible immediate successor should he, Marcos, become too ill to remain in office. The beleaguered president also announced that he would call for national parliamentary elections in the spring of 1984, even though his own term would not expire until 1987.

Many Filipinos, however, regarded these moves by the First Family as merely cosmetic—an attempt to cover up the serious blemishes that scar the face of their nation. What is needed, they say, is a completely new government that will restore democracy to the Philippines and rescue the nation's all but bankrupt economy. And to accomplish this, another revolution may be necessary.

COMMUNISTS
STILL STRONG

If there is a revolution, it may well be headed by the Communist party of the Philippines (CPP) and its military arm, the New People's Army. The NPA, however, numbers only about ten thousand guerrillas and would

be no match for the Philippine Army of several hundred thousand well-trained troops. Consequently, the CPP has tried to gain strength by making alliances with the many groups that oppose the Marcos regime. If this can be accomplished, the CPP will become a truly formidable force.

The CPP has been greatly aided in gaining new alliances by the murder of Aquino. The assassination unified members of the liberal opposition by making them realize that they must band together or be destroyed separately. The major problem facing the opposition, however, is that so far no dynamic leader has arisen to head a revolutionary takeover of the government. Aquino could well have been such a leader, especially since he had the powerful support of the United States.

Meanwhile, what the CPP as well as other Marcos opponents fear is a massive military crackdown that may be worse than that of the early 1970s, when martial law was declared. Heading this crackdown, many CPP members believe, may be General Fabian Ver, armed forces chief of staff, whom they also blame for the Aquino assassination. In any such purge, the CPP would, of course, become one of the main targets.

The future of the Philippines and the political fate of Ferdinand Marcos are difficult to predict, but with antigovernment protest demonstrations like this one becoming more and more frequent, change seems inevitable.

CORAZON AQUINO, A POSSIBLE
OPPOSITION LEADER

In the months that followed her husband's assassination, Mrs. Corazon Aquino began to emerge as a powerful behind-the-scenes leader of the Marcos opposition. A staunch anticommunist, Mrs. Aquino nevertheless advocated a continuation of the protest movement against the government. She also favored a boycott of the 1984 elections if Marcos was still president.

According to the Philippine constitution, citizens are required to vote, and those who fail to do so are liable to punishment of six months imprisonment. But early in 1984, Roman Catholic Church officials said that Filipinos could boycott the coming elections in good conscience because of the political upheavals following the assassination of opposition leader Aquino.

Mrs. Aquino said that she would refuse any open leadership role but would endorse any other strong democratic leader. She also opposed revolutionary violence, favoring instead civil disobedience, such as boycotts against the newspapers and nationwide sitdown strikes for labor reforms.

In her behind-the-scenes efforts, Mrs. Aquino was working with the Catholic Church and in particular Cardinal Jaime Sin, the Roman Catholic Archbishop of Manila.

CHURCH LEADER
OPPOSES MARCOS

Cardinal Sin has been perhaps the best known and most violent critic of the Marcos regime to emerge since the Aquino assassination. He has branded the Marcos government a "travesty of democracy" and likened it to the Nazi government under Adolf Hitler. This is strong talk coming from a former Marcos friend.

But Sin has also preached moderation, calling for a national reconciliation council to be formed as the only hope for avoiding a bloody revolution. Many observers see Sin as a bridge between the Marcos government and its opponents.

Before the Aquino murder, Cardinal Sin was only an occasional critic of the government, speaking out against bans on freedom of the press and rigged elections. Since then, he has become more militant, refusing to serve on the Agrava Commission and labeling it a sham. But at the same time, Sin has refused to throw the full weight of the Church behind the Marcos opposition. Instead, he has advanced his plan for national reconciliation.

Cardinal Sin's reconciliation plan calls for a council made up of representatives of the government and its opposition as well as members of Church and private business groups. It gives several conditions for reconciliation—free elections, a free press, and an independent judiciary. It also demands a "thorough and impartial" inquiry into the Aquino assassination.

Early in 1984, President Marcos promised to study the Sin proposal but added that he reserved the right to decide on the method of maintaining law and order in the Philippines. Meanwhile, the schism between Church and state leaders continued to widen, and Sin continued to grow in stature as the government's strongest and best-known critic.

JOSE DIOKNO, A POSSIBLE
PRESIDENTIAL CANDIDATE

If and when another presidential election is held, one person who may well become a candidate for the presidency is Jose Diokno. Diokno, a middle-aged Filipino lawyer and politician, is a long-time Marcos foe. He is also a staunch Philippine nationalist who wants no foreign interference in his country's affairs—including interference from the United States. However, he is not against accepting foreign aid—provided it has no strings attached.

Early in the Marcos regime, Diokno was jailed for two years without a trial or without having any specific charges brought against him. Diokno claims that he was just one of some seventy thousand other dissidents who were similarly detained.

When he was released from jail, Diokno formed a legal assistance group for such detainees. This group, which is still active, is made up of young law students and local village leaders who instruct people throughout the country on their legal rights.

Diokno also played a key role in a documentary film about conditions in the Philippines, produced by the British Broadcasting Company for world distribution. Called *To Sing Our Own Song*, this BBC documentary was first shown in the United States on the Public Broadcasting System early in 1984 and caused much discussion among private citizens and government officials alike.

In the documentary, Diokno charges that the Marcos government has done little to remedy Filipino unemployment, which runs as high as 25 percent. On the contrary, it has exploited it. Cheap Filipino labor, Diokno said, favors foreign governments with large investments in the Philippines. The economy thus satisfies the needs of foreign markets and well-to-do, or "elite," Filipinos.

"Too much time and money is spent by Marcos and his wife on 'image building,' " Diokno added, referring to the expensive Manila children's hospital sponsored by the First Lady, which caters to the children of the wealthy. Cardinal Sin has also criticized this hospital, referring to it as "a basilica for the rich."

"What is needed," Diokno points out, "is mass health care. As matters stand now, all good things come from above [from Marcos and his wife], not from the efforts of the people *for* the people."

In citing the need for mass health care, Diokno emphasized that dysentery is the fourth cause of death in his country. He also said that 80 percent of Filipino children under five years of age suffer from malnutrition.

Both as a humanitarian and a politician, Diokno has a special interest in the youth of his nation, since more than half the population is twenty years old or younger. Any coordinated youth movement would be a powerful national political force.

Diokno and others have also pointed out that outside the cities, in the rural Philippines, the military forces have become the government. The 300,000-man regular army has been augmented by local paramilitary groups trained by the army to exert local control. Military suppression and the terrorizing of villagers, including children, has become a way of life, according to reports from the organization, Amnesty International. Amnesty International is a nonprofit world peace organization that observes and reports on all examples of human rights violations wherever they occur. Such violations often lead to revolution and war.

FORMATION OF
THE NATIONAL
DEMOCRATIC FRONT

Largely as a matter of self-preservation, many farmers have formed guerrilla groups to fight against the military government. Some of these groups have joined together in the so-called National Democratic Front, which preaches liberation from oppression and exploitation.

Among the most militant of the members of the National Democratic Front are rice farmers who have been driven off their land in central Luzon to create what Marcos has hailed as "the largest dam and power plant in Asia." Marcos claims this project, when finished, will benefit all Filipinos by supplying them with cheap, abundant power. Diokno and his followers, however, insist that this plant and other development projects merely exploit the people for the benefit of the "multinationals" or foreign investors.

In his opposition to the multinationals, Diokno is also outspoken against what he calls "U.S. imperialism." The huge Subic Bay Naval Base, Diokno insists, not only corrupts local Filipinos and destroys their normal way of life but also threatens the whole of the Philippines because, "It is probably the main base for American atomic weapons in Asia."

Diokno's opposition to the American presence in the Philippines is by no means shared by all Filipinos, however. Among those opposed to Diokno's anti-American stance are most businessmen on the islands. They merely want a change in government, not a social revolution.

PRO-MARCOS CANDIDATES

If neither his wife, Imelda, nor military strongman Ver succeeds Marcos in office, there are several other pro-Marcos candidates for the job whom businessmen favor. These include Prime Minister Cesar Virata, an economist who is highly respected in financial circles; Rafael Sales, a former staff assistant to Marcos and now a United Nations official; Enrique Zobel, himself a leading Manila businessman; and Eduardo Cojuangco, a rich landowner who virtually controls the Philippines coconut industry.

Marcos opponent Salvador Laurel, a former senator who also has presidential aspirations, has charged that Cojuangco is a potential dictator who has already created his own thousand-man private army. Interestingly, Cojuangco is a first cousin of Mrs. Benigno Aquino, but he and Aquino were bitter political enemies, and there have been persistent rumors that Cojuangco was involved in the Aquino slaying.

It has been a matter of self-interest among these potential candidates and other Filipino business leaders to back widespread government reforms rather than support any outright attempt to overthrow the government. They are advocates of moderation because revolution would doubtless destroy or at least place in peril vast amounts of investments in and debts owed by the government. A revolution would destroy the fabric of the Filipino economy, and a communist takeover would replace the capitalist economy with state-run stores and other enterprises. Because of this, the United States has backed moderate candidates such as Enrique Zobel, who has no political experience but was close to both Aquino and Marcos.

FUTURE FINANCIAL PROBLEMS

Whoever succeeds Marcos will face formidable future financial problems. These center around the Philippines' foreign indebtedness, which threatened to climb from a staggering $22 billion to perhaps $30 billion in the mid-1980s. In an attempt to repay this debt, Marcos adopted severe economic thrift measures—devaluation of the peso by more than 21 percent, freezing wages and prices of all commodities, restricting credit, imposing strong import controls, and halting various government-sponsored development projects. He also tried to make it more difficult for rich Filipinos to take their money out of the country, as many were doing. If such a drain on Philippine banks were to continue, the country might soon be bankrupt.

Such austerity measures made a harsh life even harsher for the average Filipino, but they did bring a measure of economic stability to the Republic's economy. The International Monetary Fund (IMF), with strong support from the United States, indicated that it would continue to aid the Philippines with the refinancing of its foreign debt and perhaps additional loans. Such refinancing would make it possible for the Philippine government to pay just the interest on its foreign loans without immediately having to repay the loans themselves. The IMF, however, was keeping a watchful eye on the political stability of the Philippines.

Any prolonged nationwide strikes, anti-Marcos rallies that turned violent, open oppression by the military, or signs of a threatened government collapse might well cause the IMF to stop supporting the Philippines' badly battered economy. Should this occur, economic chaos would almost certainly follow. Not just bankers and businessmen fear such a possibility. The governments of the United States, Japan, and those of numerous European nations with large investments in and trade with the Philippines all want to avoid such an eventuality at all costs.

From time to time, President Marcos has suggested that if the free nations of the West are no longer interested in supporting the Philippines, perhaps the Soviet Union might be. Whether or not he would make good on such veiled threats is, of course, uncertain. But the United States cannot allow it to become a reality. Should that happen, it is not beyond imagining that the United States would once again militarily take over control of the Philippines.

But this is only a remote possibility. The Reagan administration has made it amply clear that the United States has a permanent stake in the Philippines Republic. The Philippines' vitally important strategic location and the two major U.S. military bases at Clark Field and

Subic Bay make the Philippines a bastion that must be maintained no matter what the cost. Doubtless, any future U.S. administration will continue to espouse the same attitude.

However, at least for the foreseeable future, the Philippines, both economically and politically will remain a major American problem in the Pacific.

AND WHAT IS
FERDINAND MARCOS'
FUTURE?

If the Philippines is the sick outpost of the Pacific, there seems to be little doubt that its leader is also far from well. U.S. diplomats as well as other observers are certain that President Marcos is in poor health, but they are uncertain about the gravity of his illness. Even some members of Marcos' own government have expressed their private dismay at his obvious physical decline and doubt that he will live until the end of his current presidential term, which technically expires in 1987. Reportedly, Marcos is suffering from a serious kidney ailment and has been given no longer than two years to live.

But the Philippines leader has steadfastly denied the truth of all statements about his illness. At a meeting with Manila businessmen late in 1983, he said that he was tired of answering questions about his health and the future of his government. "I am not going to step down, and I am not going to die," he said bluntly.

No one, least of all his political opponents, is likely to underestimate either Marcos' physical resilience or his strong standing as a result of his actions as a guerrilla fighter in both war and peace. Nor can they ignore the fact that he is still a keen and able politician. Consequently, many Filipinos fully expect him to confound his critics by outliving his enemies and playing a major role in handpicking his own successor.

With this end in view, Marcos has gone about shrewdly strengthening his current political machine, the KBL (Tagalog initials for the New Society Movement), with his eye steadfastly on the future. His opponents call Marcos' stubborn refusal to relinquish the power of his office a recipe for chaos in the Republic of the Philippines. Who will prove to be correct only the future can reveal.

BIBLIOGRAPHY

Bocca, Geoffrey. *The Philippines: America's Forgotten Friends*. Parents' Magazine, New York, 1974.

Chaffee, F.H. *Area Handbook for the Philippines*. U.S. Government Printing Office, Washington, D.C., 1979.

Freidel, Frank. *The Splendid Little War*. Little, Brown and Co., Boston, 1958.

Friend, Theodore. *Between Two Empires: The Ordeal of the Philippines, 1929–1946*. Yale University Press, New Haven, Conn. 1965.

Grunder, G.A., and W.E. Livezey. *The Philippines and the United States*. University of Oklahoma Press, Norman, OK. 1951.

Kuhn, Delia and Ferdinand. *The Philippines: Yesterday and Today*. Holt Rinehart, New York, 1966.

Lawson, Don. *The United States in the Spanish-American War*. Abelard-Schuman, New York, 1976.

_____The United States in World War II. Abelard-Schuman, New York, 1964.

MacArthur, Douglas. *Reminiscences*. McGraw-Hill Book Co., New York, 1964.

Paxton, John, ed. *The Statesman's Yearbook, 1983–84.* St. Martin's Press, New York, 1984.

Romulo, Carlos P. *I See the Philippines Rise.* Doubleday & Co., New York, 1946.

Spence, Hartzell. *For Every Tear a Victory—The Story of Ferdinand E. Marcos.* McGraw-Hill Book Co., New York, 1964.

Steinberg, Rafael. *Return to the Philippines.* Time-Life Books, Time, Inc., New York, 1980.

The World Almanac and Book of Facts. Newspaper Enterprise Association, Inc., New York, 1984.

Wolfert, Ira. *American Guerrilla in the Philippines.* Simon & Schuster, New York, 1945.

INDEX

Italicized page numbers refer to photographs.

Agrava Commission, 5, 69, 70, 75
Agriculture, 13–14, 19–23
Aguinaldo, Emilio, 45, 47, 49–50
Aquino, Agapito, 5, 70
Aquino, Benigno "Ninoy," 16, 18, 35–37, 68; assassination of, 1–6, 69–70, 73, 75
Aquino, Corazon, 37, 74, 79

Balang, Ramon, 69–70
Bonifacio, Andrés, 45

Cam Ranh Bay, 9–10
Cebu, island, 11, 13, 43
China, 43, 44
Clark Air Force Base, 8–9, 10, 80
Cojuangco, Eduardo, 78–79
Communism, 4, 5, 25–27, 67, 68, 79
Communist party of the Philippines (CPP), 71–73
Cuba, 46, 49

Dewey, George, 46, 47
Dimailig, Carlito, 41
Diokno, Jose, 75–77, 78

Economy, 22, 71, 79, 80
Elections, 15, 16, 18, 74

Family life, 19–24
Farming, 13–14, 19–23
Fernando, Enrique M., 4
Free Men, 31–32, 59–63
Funston, Frederick, 52–55

Galman, Rolando, 1–3, 5–6, 69–70
Garcia, Carlos P., 68
Government, 14–18, 22, 25, 33–35, 40. *See also* Marcos regime

Health, 22, 77
Herrera, Ernesto, 70
Housing, 19, 24
Huk rebellion, 35, 67, 68

International Monetary Fund (IMF), 80

Japan, WWII invasion and occupation of Philippines, 14, 31, 58–66

Katipunan movement, 45
KBL, 82

Languages, 14
Laurel, José P., 59
Laurel, Salvador, 78
Leyte, island, 11, 64, *65*
Liberal party, 16, 33, 36
Luzon, island, 8, 11, 59, 78

Macapagal, Diosdado, 68
MacArthur, Arthur, 50–53, 60
MacArthur, Douglas, 32, 52, 60–*65*, 67
McKinley, William, 47–49, 52
Magsaysay, Ramon, 68
Manila, 13, 24, 62, *66*, 67
Marcos, Ferdinand Edralin, 29–42 *and illus.*, 81–82; early life of, 29–30; early political career, 32–33; and Free Men, 31–32, 59, 61, 62, 63; and World War II, 31–32
Marcos, Imelda Romualdez, 36, 37–41, 71, 78
Marcos regime, 16–18, 35–37, 81–82; and Aquino assassination, 1–6, 70; and NPA, 25–27, 35, 71–73; opposition to, 2, 4, 5, 6, 15, 17, 70, 71; relations with U.S., 5, 6–9, 79, 80–81
Martial law, 2, 16, 18

National Democratic Front, 77–78
Nationalist party, 16, 33
New People's Army (NPA), 25–27, 35, 71–73

Osmena, Sergio, 58
Otis, Elwell S., 50–52

Philippine Army, 73, 77
Philippines, Common-
wealth of the, 58
Philippines, Republic of
the; climate, 13; Con-
stitutions of, 2, 15–16;
democracy in, 2, 4, 16,
18, 35; early history of,
43–55; foreign aid to,
6–7, 21, 35, 79; geogra-
phy of, 11; government
of, 14–18, 22, 25, 33–
35, 40; independence
of, 15, 67; islands of,
11; Japanese invasion
and occupation of, 14,
31, 58–64, 66; popula-
tion of, 11, 13, 14, 19,
22; United States con-
trol of, 14–15, 48, 49–
57. *See also* Marcos re-
gime
Propaganda Movement,
44–45

Quezon, Manuel L., 58,
60, 67
Quirino, Elpidio, 67, 68

Raval, Vicente, 61
Reagan, Ronald, 5, 6, 7,
80
Regalado, Reuben, 69

Religion, 14, 26, 43, 44,
74
Rizal, José B., 37, 44–45
Roman Catholicism, 14,
26, 44, 74
Roosevelt, Theodore, 46,
55
Roxas, Manuel, 67

Sales, Rafael, 78
Segismundo, Cecilio, 53–
55
Sin, Jaime Cardinal, 74–
75, 76
Soviet Union, 8, 9–10, 80
Spanish-American War,
14, 46–48, 49
Spanish colonization of
Philippines, 43–49
Subic Bay Naval Base, 8,
9, 10, 78, 81

Taft, William Howard, 52,
53, 57
Tatad, Francisco, 40, 41
To Sing Our Own Song, 76

Tolentino, Arturo, 5
Tydings-McDuffie Act, 57

United States; aid to
Phil., 6–7, 21, 35, 79;
control of Phil., 14–15,
48, 49–57; relations
with Marcos regime, 5,
6–9, 79, 80–81

U.S. military forces, 7, 8, 9, 10, *48*, 50–53, 61, 63, 64, 78, 80

Ver, Fabian, 73, 78

Vietnam, and war, 9–10

Virata, Cesar, 78

World War II, 14, 31–32, 58–64

Zobel, Enrique, 78, 79